Enid Blyton's

·BIBLE·STORIES·

A PATH THROUGH THE SEA
THE SEA
& BREAD FROM THE SKY

OLD TESTAMENT
BOOK 8

GRANADA PUBLISHING

A PATH THROUGH THE SEA

Moses led the people of Egypt to the shores of the Red Sea. God put a pillar of cloud in the sky by day to show them the way, and at night he put a pillar of flame.

Pharaoh was angry when the slaves had gone. Who would do the work they had done? "They have gone in safety, taking their flocks with them, and much of our gold," said Pharaoh.

His spies answered him. "Lord, we have watched the slaves where they go, and they are now on the shores of the Red Sea. Send your army after them, and you will trap them there."

So Pharaoh gave orders that six hundred of his swiftest chariots should gallop after the slaves, and behind these chariots should come others, with the Egyptian army following.

"We will kill all the slaves," said the king, "and we will take from them all their belongings and our gold."

Now the slaves were camping by the Red Sea. Before them lay a wild, unknown country. Beside them was the sea. In the sky was the great pillar of cloud that guided them.

Suddenly one of the slaves saw a cloud of dust in the distance. What could it be? The people called to one another, and pointed to it.

"Many people must be coming," they said. "Surely it cannot be the Egyptians."

The cloud of dust was made by the chariots of Pharaoh's army. Six hundred of them were galloping after the slaves.

Then Moses heard the thunder of the horses' hoofs, and the rumbling of the chariot wheels. He knew that Pharaoh had sent his army, and he was afraid. The slaves were in

4

great fear too, and cried out to Moses.

"Where shall we go? The wild country is beyond us, and the sea bars our way."

"Do not fear," said Moses. "The Lord God will save us."

Moses went down to the sea and prayed to

God to help him, and God answered him at once.

"Tell my people not to fear, for they shall go on their way. Lift up your staff, Moses, and put out your hand over the sea, and divide the waters in two. My people shall walk in the midst of the sea on dry land. Then will the Egyptians know that I am the Lord God."

Moses put his hand out over the sea, and lifted up his staff. Then there came a strong wind, bellowing from the east, making enormous waves on the sea.

All through the night the strong wind blew, and it was very cold. The slaves were frightened and restless, knowing that they would be attacked in the morning.

The wind blew back the waters of the sea as the tide went out. It piled up the waters and divided them, so that a pathway of dry land showed in the midst of the sea.

The slaves were full of wonder the next morning when daylight came, and showed them the strange pathway through the waves. They gazed down it, seeing the walls of steep water on each side, held back by the wind. Here was their way of escape.

"Come, my people," said Moses. This is the way that the Lord God has made for us. Bring your flocks and herds and follow me."

Then the people, with their children and their flocks and herds, went down to the pathway that divided the waters. They walked on it through the sea. The way was not easy, for the cold wind still blew and the people shivered; the path was full of pools and sometimes quicksands, for it had only yesterday been the bottom of the sea.

But the escaping slaves walked steadily

across the pathway, and came to the other
side, where they were safe.

The Egyptians awoke and sent out their
spies to see what the slaves had done in the
night. The men came back with a strange tale.

"The slaves are gone!" they said. "Their flocks and herds are gone too. They have walked through the midst of the sea."

"What tale is this!" cried the captains.

"Sirs, the sea is divided in two, and there is a wide path through it," said the spies. "The slaves have taken this path and they have escaped us."

The captains were full of dismay. Pharaoh would punish them if they did not kill the slaves. "Sound the trumpets, and we will go after them!" they cried.

Then all the Egyptians leapt into their chariots and galloped to the shores of the Red Sea. They saw the wide pathway through it.

"Sir, the wind has gone, and the sky is dark," said an Egyptian to his captain. "There is a storm coming."

"On, after the slaves!" cried the captain.

"On, before the pathway goes!"

And through the midst of the sea, down the same path that the slaves had taken, went the Egyptian chariots. The men lashed their horses to make them go fast – but the heavy chariots stuck in the sand. Their wheels broke off. The horses could not gallop far in the wet sand.

The tide was coming in again. Water filled the little pools and made them big. It made the sand sink even more beneath the weight of the oncoming army. Soon the men in front could go no farther, and they leapt from their sinking chariots and tried to make their way back.

But more and more chariots came on, and the men could go neither forward nor backward. The army was in great trouble, and no one knew where to turn.

Then Moses once more stretched out his hand over the sea. The walls of water rushed

together, and the frightened Egyptians saw
them coming. They could not escape. In a few
moments there was no pathway through the
waters – the sea had gone back to its place,
and not one Egyptian was to be seen.

So once again the slaves were saved, and
they praised the Lord God as they went on
their way.

BREAD FROM THE SKY

Moses was taking the people to the Land of Canaan, the beautiful country that God had promised they should have. It was not really very far, but the people had to be taught many lessons before they could have a home of their own.

So they were a long time on the way, for they went through wild country, bare and stony, and they camped for a long time in many places.

They were an impatient people, who grumbled often, and found fault with Moses. They even grumbled against God, who had brought them out of Egypt.

One day the people camped in a bare spot, and they were very hungry. There was little food for them, and they grumbled bitterly.

They went to Moses and spoke angrily to him. "Why did you bring us out of Egypt? There at least we had good bread and meat to eat. We shall starve in this place."

Moses spoke with God, and God told him a strange thing. "I will rain bread from heaven for you."

Now each morning the dew fell. The ground became wet, and then the hot sun dried it. The next day the dew fell as it always did, and the people took no notice of it, for it was a thing they saw daily.

The sun came up and dried the dew – and lo, something was left behind on the ground wher the dew had gone.

The children playing around the camp saw this strange new thing and ran to pick it up. It looked rather like hoar-frost to them.

"Look!" cried the children. "What is this

white stuff all over the grass? We have never seen it before."

The people looked at it and picked it up.

It was small and white and round. What could it be?

"This is manna, bread from heaven," said the people in joy.

"It is the bread which the Lord God sends you to eat," said Moses. "It is his gift to you.

It will melt when the sun is high, so gather it now and eat it. Each one can take as much as he can eat."

The children ran to gather the manna, and they brought it to their parents. Everyone ate it with joy, for it tasted like wafers made with honey.

"Bread from the sky!" said the children, in wonder. "Truly the Lord God looks after his people."

Another time the people camped in a wild place and could find no water to drink. No matter how they searched around, there was no stream, no spring, no pool to be found.

Then they were thirsty and they grumbled loudly. "Now we have no water to drink! We shall die of thirst, and our children too."

They went to Moses and were angry with him. "See, we die of thirst!" they said. "Did you bring us out of Egypt for this? Give us water to drink!"

The people spoke so fiercely that Moses was afraid. He went apart and prayed to God.

"Lord, tell me what to do with this people. They are so thirsty that they are ready to stone me if I do not give them water."

Then the Lord God gave Moses his answer, and Moses was glad.

"There is a big rock in Horeb," said the Lord. "Take the people there, and take your staff with you. Strike the rock, and behold, I will make water gush forth so that the people may drink."

Moses went back to his grumbling people. He took them to the great rock and stood before it. He lifted his staff and struck the rock with it – and behold, there came water that gushed out of the rock, and ran down to the ground in bright streams.

Then the people brought their cups and
dishes, and took what water they wanted for
drinking and washing. They were no longer

thirsty, and once again they followed Moses with trust and joy.

After a long time they came to a great high mountain, whose top was in the clouds. Thunder came down from it, and the people trembled,

thinking that their Lord God was there.

"The Lord wishes to speak with me," said Moses, and he began to climb up the mountain. Thunder rolled with a sound of trumpets, and the watching people were afraid. Surely God was in the mountain that day!

"Moses goes to meet our God," said the people to one another, and they waited patiently for him to come back.

After some hours their leader came down the mountain. He brought with him two great flat pieces of stone. On them were written ten commandments.

"See, here are commandments given to me by God, for you to hear and obey," said Moses. I will read them to you, and you must for ever afterwards obey them. They are God's own words to his people."

Then Moses read out the ten commandments,

and the people promised to obey them, though many times they forgot, and did wrong.

Again Moses went up into the mountain, for God wished once more to speak to his chosen leader.

This time the Lord told Moses to make him a wonderful tent, a holy tent that should be his own dwelling-place.

"I will come to my holy tent, and I will be near to my chosen people," said the Lord. "Take my tent with you wherever you go, so that I may be with you."

Moses told the people, and with joy they set to work to make a beautiful tent for their God to dwell in so that he would be in the midst of his people. Everyone brought gold and silver and beautiful jewels to help to make a magnificent dwelling-place, the people's first church, for their Lord God.

They made a wonderful tent, and carried it with them wherever they went, their Holy Place, their church, the dwelling-place of the spirit of God.

And then at length, after forty years, they came to the fair land of Canaan. They settled there in happiness, glad to have a country of their own at last.

·THE·END·